Mind Poems

Alan Starkie

chapter one . . . Believe

See you tomorrow	6
Do something	8
The sun always follows the moon	10
Pale blue dot	12
Walk the path	14
Safe and warm	16
Step forward	18

chapter two . . . Be

Please take it	22
Be	24
Don't take yourself for granted	26
Criticisms raised	28
Northern Lights over Northern houses	30
Questions	32

chapter three . . . Love

(True meanings)	36
Moment of leaving	38
Love	40
Life is a memory	42
Happy bones	44
Uninvited dreams	46

chapter four . . . Acceptance

I spoke to Katy	50
Relativity	52
The card has been dealt	54
A moment in a tear	56
Age	58
The very last day	60
Just a seed	62

chapter five . . . One last thing

Little things	66

Copyright © 2024 Alan Starkie
All rights reserved.

chapter one

Believe

see you tomorrow

Good morning to you
Nice to see you again
Let's hope for a day
That doesn't depend
On taking what's said
Like the world's not a friend
Let's just get along
And get to the end

Good evening to us
A good day I hope
Was had without mayhem
We know we can cope
You're loved and you're needed
I've told you before
But in case you've forgotten
I'll tell you once more

Good night dear friend
You've made it again
Be proud of the person
You are and remain
The fighter, the lover
The believer of others
Now get some rest
And I'll see you tomorrow

do something

Take a moment, take a breath
Do something that won't increase your wealth
Something pointless with no applause
Do it now, don't think, don't pause

Do something unimportant
Of no use to anyone else
Something that only matters
To you, your inner self

Do something that has no purpose
Entirely out of the blue
And when it's done, enjoy the fact
You did it just for you

the sun always follows the moon

If you disagree, say something
If it's important, just be heard
When life gets too fast, take a breath
The antidote to sadness is a problem shared

If the day's too much, let me know
If the night's too dark, find some light
Feeling lonely doesn't mean you're alone
If you're wrong, I'll try to make you right

You'll be okay, I know you will
Just step out of the room
Darkness is just a fleeting moment
Because the sun always follows the moon

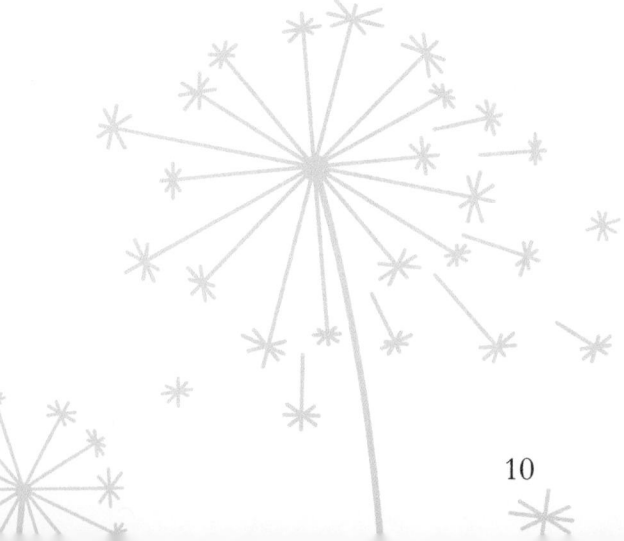

pale blue dot

You can stand in one place
For an entire lifetime
And move the same distance
As everyone else

You can sing the same song
Over and over to different people
But for each new listener
There's a connection with themselves

Points of view and movement
Are always relative to what's familiar
The Pale Blue Dot never changes
In the lens that takes the picture

Doing nothing or going nowhere
And yet doing everything and never ceasing
We live, we die but we're never still
We never stop moving
And we never will

You can stand in one place
For an entire lifetime
And move the same distance
As everyone else

You can sing the same song
Over and over to different people
But for each new listener
There's a connection with themselves

Points of view and movement
Are always relative to what's familiar
The Pale Blue Dot never changes
In the lens that takes the picture

Doing nothing or going nowhere
And yet doing everything and never ceasing
We live, we die but we're never still
We never stop moving
And we never will

walk the path

Walk the path that's true to you
Bad days occur but hopefully few
Be the judge of your happiness
You decide if it makes you less

Walk the path and lead the way
Wave goodbye to yesterday
Pull the weak into your arms
And let the children feel your calm

Walk the path that hurts sometimes
The greater good has jagged lines
That cut your feet and break your heart
Don't fear the fall from the apple cart

Walk the path no matter what speed
Drag yourself, will yourself, never concede
Take everyone who believes in your cause
Don't let them down, they'll be your applause

safe and warm

When you open your eyes to a titanic wreck
Just remember you're safe and warm in bed
When it's so dark and bleak and you can
Taste the rust from the rotting hull
Just remember you're safe and warm and in your bed

When the sheer size of a long dead ship
Pulls you in to never refloat
Remember that you're safe and warm in your bed

When you feel crushed by the miles of water
Above your head
Bearing down in your dreams turning the water red
Just remember
You're always safe and warm and in your bed

step forward

Start planning a plan, a plan of action
To overthrow overthinking reactions
A new rule of thumb leading the way
Thinking that ensures the mind doesn't stray

Add new depth to the voice that keeps saying
Step forward, step forward, the path you are taking
Breathe it all in, fresh weather's approaching
Lifting the wings of the birds as they're hoping

For better winds to tomorrow's adventure
So easy to find but so difficult to enter
Air columns that lead you away from old life
That threatened to change truth for cheap lies

The time to this point, you were destined to follow
Unnatural confusion is a heart full of sorrow
Feelings of debt for a bet never placed
A feeling now gone, now redundant, replaced

By the desire to be an anchor for the unsteady
Of which you were one but now stand here ready
For what is to come and what now has been
Step forward, step forward, be brave and be seen

chapter two

please take it

If I offer you help please take it
If I offer you love please feel it
If I offer you something
That isn't useful right now
Just hide it away until needed

If you tell me a secret I'll keep it
In a safe place where no-one can find it
All the things that are mine
Little trinkets of time
All the worthless regrets
That you help me unwind

I can only say thank you
And return in kind
If I offer you help
Please take it

be

Be the torch, be the fuse
Shine a light on someone bruised
In the dark, on the floor
Crawling round to find the door

Be the hand that they feel
Give them hope and make it real
Be the sign that leads them home
Back to the world they thought was gone

Be the words they need to hear
Make them see that help is near
Be the look that makes it right
And be the voice that says good night

don't take yourself for granted

Don't take yourself for granted
You're a person, not a machine
Machines are cogs and numbers
Unliving components gleaned
From human ideas to completion
Nothing to something to dust
Humans remain as memories
Machines end up as rust

Don't take yourself for granted
You bleed when you are cut
Whether seen or hidden away
Your pain cannot be shut
Inside a metal heart
Or compiled to binary code
You're a living breathing form
On an old and beaten road

Don't take yourself for granted
Life is more than data
Ones and zeros calculated
To make you feel it's later
Than what it actually is
We only need each other
Don't take yourself for granted
A machine is not another

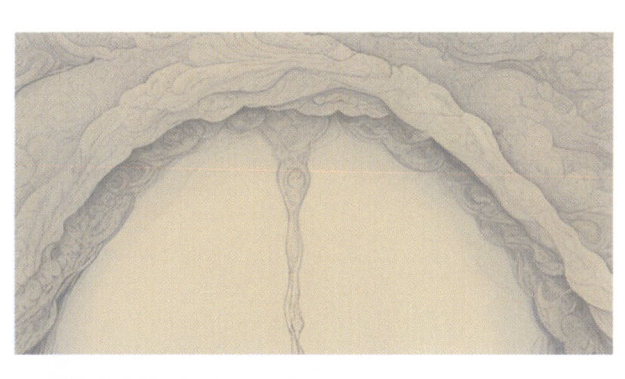

criticisms raised

I awoke to find myself
In the foulest of moods
I'd spent all night
Concocting a feud
With a person who didn't
Exist before bed
I'd turned off the lights
But didn't power-down my head

It didn't take long
For the day to arrive
The morning woke up
And I opened my eyes
Who was that person
Who knew all that I know?
The ins and the outs
The stops and the gos

I couldn't reply
To criticisms raised
He seemed to know
All the right things to say
How the hell could he know
What I wanted to be?
It soon became clear
He's not him, he's just me

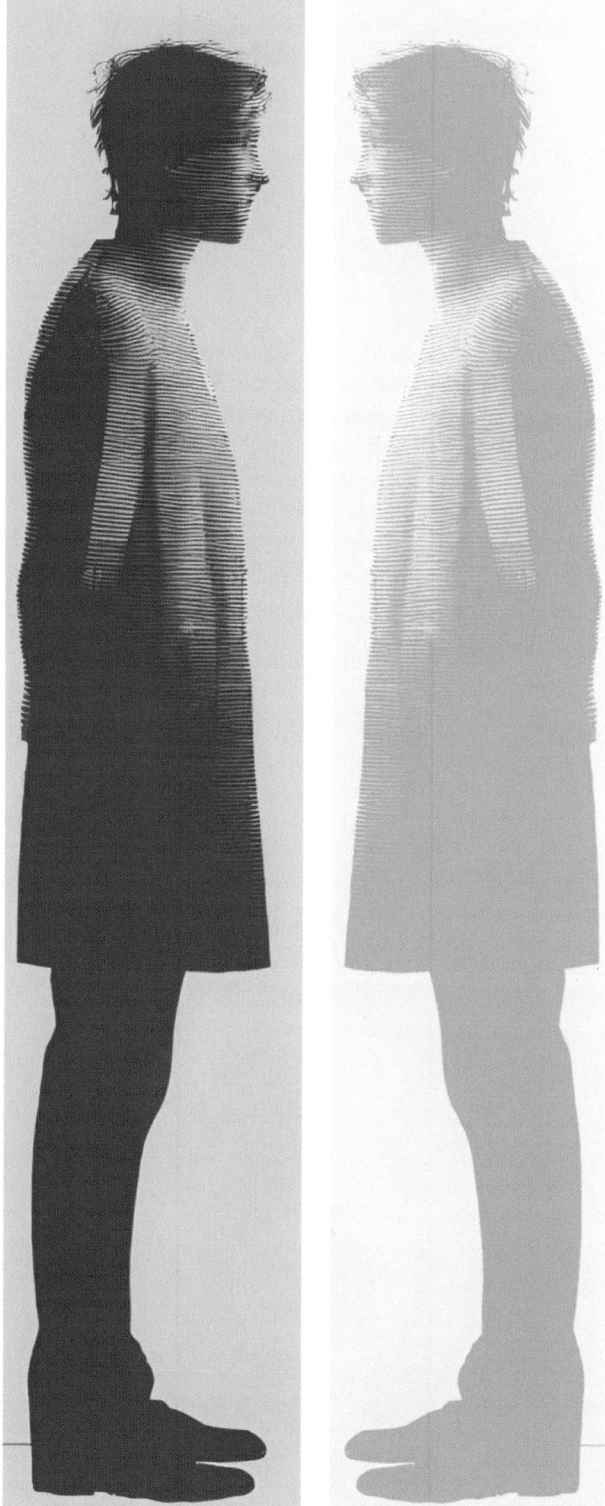

northern lights over northern houses

I didn't know the Northern Lights
Were over my northern house last night
I stepped outside hoping to see
But the aurora borealis had already been

So I took in the immenseness of the night
And decided I hadn't missed a thing
As it's still there, the sun touching the earth
Oblivious to the fact that I'm watching

questions

If you think you've hurt my feelings
Please remind me that you've not
My wires are just so tangled
One of my many faults

If I try too hard to please you
But appear underwhelmed at best
Ironically saying how less is more
Whilst overindulged more or less

My shortfalls are the human mind
The mind in question mine
Questions, questions, questions
Queueing up in question lines

If you come across an answer
Regardless of the theme
Please CC me in an email
And we can pretend we're in a team

chapter three

(true meanings)

We don't care what is said
(We do, it really hurts)
We laugh off accusations of intentions
(We don't, we're trying desperately to smile)

Sticks and stones may break our bones
But words cut deeper than knives
We move forward and brush aside the pain
(We don't, we just try to survive)

moment of leaving

If you're missing the love
Of a loved one now gone
Take a moment alone
And decide to become

The keeper of that spirit
Who loved you so much
That at the moment of leaving
They entrusted their love

To you to hold safe
And never let go
And continue to share
The love of that soul

love

You make my mind work
In the strangest of ways
I become distracted
Thinking of words to say

You affect me excessively
There's no middle ground
My thoughts are deafening
But without any sound

I struggle to stay upright
You intoxicate my heart
Beating ever faster
The end becomes the start

Time may run to nothing
And everything disappear
But love remains eternal
Forever real, forever here

life is a memory

A memory is an elusive friend
Who turns up unannounced
There is no knock, it walks right in
Hidden once, now found

A moment of profound awareness
Unshareable, unseen, a loner
Never to be known or felt
By anyone but the owner

There is no proof it ever left
No proof it ever came
Feeling like a long lost friend
Never to be heard again

If the day seems like a heavy weight
Make the good outweigh the bad
Because everything else is a memory
What we have will eventually be had

happy bones

I don't care what you've got
I'll still hold you
If we both die together
I've still got you

It's the perfect storm
An eternal win-win
A situation that I'm happy to be in

If you feel you're alone
Don't worry, my bones
Will wrap around yours when life's over

uninvited dreams

I saw you again
Out and about last night
It's been some time
Since I last caught sight
Of you walking around town
Without a care in the world
Suspended in time
Not saying a word

It was surprising to see you
There weren't any songs
But there you were waiting
In a place long since gone
You told me your problem
You had nowhere to stay
No time to find it
No place in today

So we walked to the bridge
And went our separate ways
You back to the past
And me back to today

chapter four

Acceptance

I spoke to Katy

I spoke to Katy, we needed to speak
Something had changed and I was in receipt
Of a body still here but a heart that had left
I needed to speak to Katy

I spoke to Katy, the colours had gone
My mind held my hand up to block out the sun
I couldn't stop asking what had I done?
And so I spoke to Katy

Katy replied let yourself fall
Besides this single moment
There's nothing at all
There is no tomorrow and yesterday's gone
Heartache won't end but acceptance will come

So I gave her a pebble to look at sometimes
That had travelled a millennia waiting to find
Katy right here in this moment in time
I spoke to Katy

relativity

I'm relatively rich
And relatively poor
I'm relatively sweet
But relatively sour

I'm relatively popular
And relatively unknown
Relatively relatable
Relatively alone

I'm relatively wonderful
A one-in-a-million friend
But relatively insular
And bitter to the end

Whatever you like to think you are
The opposite also applies
Because people are seen differently
Through different people's eyes

the card has been dealt

Pick a card and hold it close
The card will show what you love most
It feels your heart and knows your mind
And things in life you're yet to find

Don't fear the card, it's found it's home
It's you, the one, yourself alone
You had no choice, the card was dealt
Everything you feel has already been felt

This life isn't new, I think we all know
That whatever arrives must eventually go
There's no supernatural path to be found
Just try to move forwards towards the sound

Of cards being shuffled and cut for the masses
For drunkards and dreamers with long-empty glasses
Hoping and desperately longing to feel
That they were always part of the eventual deal

a moment in a tear

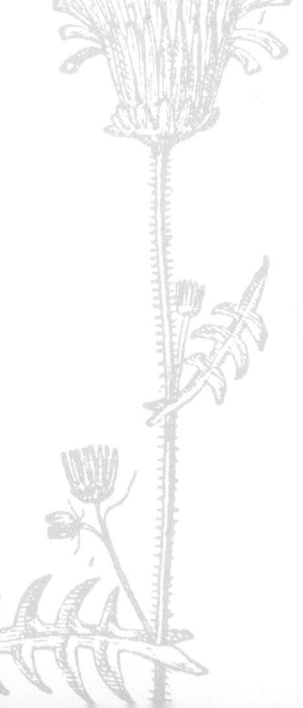

Happiness can only be felt
If you recognise the bad
Riches count for nothing
Without losing all you have

A life filled with love
Will start from an arid plain
To feel safe you must know fear
To be content requires some pain

To live life is to realise
One day you won't be here
You'll be no more and you'll be no less
Than just a moment in a tear

age

Don't fret about your age
It's the only one you have
It's the undefeated champion
Contenders make it laugh

Attempts to push it back
It sees as comedy gold
It's doing you a favour
Trying to make you old

We fight it with our vanity
Try to keep it out of sight
As if growing old and wobbly
Was something not quite right

So love your age as it loves you
And try to hold on tight
You'll be the last to see the flicker
When age turns off the light

the very last day

The mind is a box
Of infinite size
Somewhere to rest
When closing your eyes
A telephone exchange
Of forgotten calls
An ocean contained
Without any walls

A wilderness lost
In the tiniest space
With time stretching out
At an ever-faster pace
Recognising nothing
Whilst nothing calls out
Silence delayed
And muffled throughout

Sounds of the past
No longer of use
Gone but for flashes
Of split second youth
Becoming less relevant
As bodies decay
But erupting like birds
On the very last day

just a seed

I went to bed and closed my eyes
Felt the coolness of the night
Stretched out my arms to feel the sheets
That wrapped around my tired feet

The night-time clouds we never see
Sent down some rain to visit me
Tapping and fidgeting on the window pane
Not wanting to leave but unable to remain

I drifted away to the place I know best
Floating along as I do when I rest
Everyone falling but no one aware
Because people in dreams don't fall anywhere

I opened my eyes to the sky looking in
Blowing the seeds from the trees to their friends
We're just a seed of something much bigger
The clouds to the rain to the stream to the river

chapter five

One Last Thing

little things

There's a little bird
On a little branch
In a little tree
In a little park

In a little town
Filled with little people
Saying little words
That make little sounds

Blowing little breezes
That make little circles
Making little journeys
Travelling little distances

Back to little birds
On little branches
In little trees

Appreciate the little things
Before the little things leave

Believe...

Pick up a pen.
Don't think.
Write.

_____

_____

_____

_____

_____

_____

_____

_____

something of
importance
only to you

Be...

Pick up a pen.
Don't think.
Write.

_____

_____

_____

_____

_____

_____

_____

_____

something of
importance
only to you

Love...

Pick up a pen.
Don't think.
Write.

_____

_____

_____

_____

_____

_____

_____

something of
importance
only to you

Acceptance...

Pick up a pen.
Don't think.
Write.

_____

_____

_____

_____

_____

_____

_____

_____

something of
importance
only to you

Printed in Great Britain
by Amazon

c6057377-f706-49da-a11a-4f9cbd4b4134R01